WILDFLOWERS
of Southwestern Utah

A Field Guide to Bryce Canyon, Cedar Breaks
and Surrounding Plant Communities

Dr. Hayle Buchanan

Library of Congress Catalog Card Number 92-70128

ISBN 1-56044-074-0

First edition 1974
Second edition 1979
Revised edition 1992
   Reprinted 1997

Printed in Hong Kong

Published by the Bryce Canyon Natural History Association, Inc., Bryce Canyon National Park, Bryce Canyon, Utah 84717, in cooperation with SkyHouse Publishers, an imprint of Falcon® Publishing Co., Inc., Helena, Montana

Design, typesetting, and other prepress work by Falcon Graphics, Helena, Montana

Chapter head illustrations by Laurie gigette Gould

Photographs by Eugene G. Bozniak, unless otherwise noted

Illustrations by Dr. Hayle Buchanan

Distributed by Falcon® Publishing Co., Inc., P.O. Box 1718, Helena, Montana 59624, or call 1-800-582-2665

CONTENTS

Key Codes:

CB   Plants described in the plant communities of Bryce Canyon
         that also occur at Cedar Breaks.

BC   Plants described in the plant communities of Cedar Breaks
         that also occur at Bryce Canyon.

Preface

his revised edition includes updated plant taxonomy changes and almost all new photographs, in addition to some changes in the text itself. The book has served as a guide for many lovers of wildflowers who have visited scenic southern Utah during the past seventeen years since the book first appeared in print.

Appreciation and gratitude are extended by many people who have helped in the preparation of this book. The superintendents, rangers, and naturalists of Bryce Canyon National Park and Cedar Breaks National Monument have been very cooperative in many ways. Botanists have offered their suggestions and expertise in taxonomy. The photographers have spent many hours during the summer flowering seasons obtaining the excellent photographs.

I wish to express appreciation to my wife, Melva, who accompanied me on many research and collecting trips in the scenic areas of southern Utah. Her keen insight, interest, and patience have been valuable to me in making this book possible.

Dr. Hayle Buchanan
August 1991

Purpose and Description of the Book

his book has been prepared as an aid to the person who is fascinated by nature and wishes to recognize some of the wildflowers and other plant life of the higher mountain country of southern Utah. An ecological approach is used in presenting the material to help the reader gain an understanding and appreciation of the plants ''at home'' in their own natural communities.

The plants are arranged in eight representative communities. These communities are grouped in a sequence beginning just above the foothill forests of pinyon-juniper and extending upward to and beyond timberline. Each of the eight communities is introduced by a full-page, colored, aspect photograph accompanied by a brief analysis of the ecological factors that support that particular community. Following this, representative plants of the community are illustrated individually and described as to the common name, the Latin botanical name, the English form of the family name, certain distinctive characteristics of the plant, habitat requirements of the plant, niche or role of the plant in the community, Native American uses of products of the plant, pioneer uses of products of the plant, and other pertinent information.

Taxonomists have classified several hundred species of plants of Bryce Canyon National Park and Cedar Breaks National Monument. It was necessary to limit this book to a representative selection of the more common, dominant, and attractive species. However, a goodly number of the inconspicuous but important species of plants have been included to show that other things matter besides a burst of color or large size.

The typical book on wildflowers is restricted to showy herbaceous plants. This book considers the wildflowers as members of communities. If the community is a forest, the wildflowers have interrelations with the trees of the forest, which often dominate and control the other plants in their understory. Consequently, the trees of southern Utah are included in the book.

In this revised edition, line drawings of wildflowers are included, in addition to the photographs, as an aid to identification. The line drawing of a wildflower typically shows several features of the plant that are not evident in the photograph, such as shape and relative size of basal leaves, details of flower structure, and size proportions of plant parts. It is hoped that the line drawing will supplement the photograph in helping to identify and appreciate each plant species included in the book. Photographs of the basic tree shapes and closeups of their needles and cones are also included.

Visitors to the scenic mountain country of southern Utah should realize the delicate nature of a natural plant community. The wildflowers and trees can often withstand the many adversities of nature but may not survive the thoughtless practices of humans. Native plants should never be wantonly collected or destroyed. Observe them, appreciate them, photograph them, and then leave them "at home" in their own communities for others to come and enjoy. Most wildflowers cannot be transplanted successfully. These plants need environmental conditions that are difficult or impossible to duplicate in gardens. Other plants can be transplanted and easily grown in gardens, but they must not be collected from national parks and national monuments for this purpose. Hunt them with a camera and then relive your trip to the mountains by viewing the photographs you took and by looking at the illustrations of this book.

Vegetational Belts in Southern Utah's Colorful Mountain Country

 outhern Utah is characterized by many high plateaus that have been shoved and pushed to varying elevations by movements deep in the earth's interior. These high plateaus are considered mountains, not only because of the elevation and the rugged topography of their margins, but also because of the kinds of plants that cover them. Climate is dependent upon the length of season, variable conditions of moisture, prevailing wind, temperature, and light. Climate is the chief factor in deciding where plants of any given species can grow and propagate. Soil type also influences plant growth and propagation, often excluding species from an area where the climate may be favorable for its existence. Soil is generally a minor influence, however.

Roughly speaking, for every 1,000 feet of elevation, there is a drop in temperature of 3° F. Going up a mountain 1,000 feet is equivalent in climatic change to traveling northward 600 miles at the same elevation. Consequently, the plant life is arranged into vegetational belts, or life zones, on a mountainside in a pattern similar to the latitudinal zonation of plant life from the equator to the poles. These zones of life seldom have sharp boundaries, but tend to intergrade into each other. A particular vegetational belt attains its characteristic development within certain altitudinal limits, but there are often extensions up or down the mountain, depending upon local changes in slope steepness, slope direction, moisture, and mineral conditions of the soil.

Within the region covered by this book, the elevation of the mountains varies from 6,500 feet to over 11,000 feet. The wildflower enthusiast who learns to recognize the vegetational belts by identifying a relatively few dominant plants will soon discover that he can expect to find certain wildflowers in a specific belt or life zone. As his knowledge of plants develops, he will be able to locate new flowers and also identify unfamiliar ones. The eight plant communities of this book fit into five vegetational belts as follows:

   I . Bryce Canyon Breaks Community:
      Pinyon-Juniper Woodland Belt

  II. Ponderosa Pine Forest:
     Submontane Forest Belt

 III. High Plateau Sagebrush Community:
     Submontane Forest Belt

 IV. Fir-Spruce-Aspen Forest:
    Montane Forest Belt

  V. Subalpine Open, Semi-Moist Meadows:
    Subalpine Forest Belt

 VI. Subalpine Marshy Meadows:
    Subalpine Forest Belt

VII. Timberline Forest:
    Subalpine Forest Belt

VIII. Alpine Tundra on Brian Head:
     Alpine Tundra Belt

The amount of soil moisture present is probably the most important factor in determining the time, extent, and profusion of the wildflower show during a given spring and summer season. Blooming seasons of wildflowers are correlated with latitude or altitude. Within certain limits, one can travel upward on a mountain and find flowers that typically bloom "earlier" than expected, as compared with those blooming at the lower elevation. On a particular day in July, for example, one can travel by automobile from the foothills east of Bryce Canyon where the vegetation is "late summer" and arrive at Cedar Breaks a few hours later to find the "springtime" condition of vegetation. At 10,300 feet elevation, the growing season is telescoped into a few short months.

The Struggle for Plant Survival on the Bryce Canyon "Breaks"

It would be difficult to imagine a more adverse environment for plant growth than is found among the steep, eroded, pink cliffs of Bryce Canyon National Park. This cliff community of plant life is also known as the "breaks" community. Breaks is an early settlers' term for badlands. The peculiar "raindrop" erosion at Bryce Canyon has created a great variety of geologic formations and delicate scenery. For the study of plant life, the variety of slope characteristics defies classification. Surfaces vary in steepness from vertical to almost level and slope in every direction. The exposed ridges that receive the direct rays of the sun at midday represent one habitat extreme, whereas the protected, shady nooks that are heavily vegetated provide the opposite habitat extreme.

The rapid erosion of many of these slopes makes survival very difficult for very hardy species and impossible for others. The rapid erosion that creates the fantastic formations of Bryce Canyon causes special difficulties for survival and reproduction of most plant species. The roots of the plants are either undermined as erosion cuts both horizontally and vertically, or the trunks of the trees and the stems of smaller plants are covered with thick mud and rocks as the eroding material is deposited downslope by the water from summer thunderstorms or the melting snow in springtime. Even seedlings and small saplings are sometimes completely covered during severe erosion and consequently never live to maturity.

For several months in the spring and again in the fall of the year, daily freezing and thawing of water in the soil and in cracks in the rocks causes expansion and contraction of rock material. The perennial plants must tolerate these violent forces around their root systems during these seasons of the year. Alternating with the periods of violent flash floods following thunderstorms of the summer season are long periods of drought or water deficit. The high temperature and low relative humidity of the air cause rapid water loss through direct evaporation from the soil and through transpiration from the plants during most of the growing season.

The medium in which the roots of these hardy species of plants are anchored could hardly be called soil because of its lack of humus, its compaction and consequent poor aeration, the low water yield for plant processes, the paucity of soil microorganisms, the dehydrating winds, and the extreme soil temperatures. Requisites for survival of these canyon plants are inherent hardiness and tolerance to the many adversities of climate and soil conditions.

The plants of the breaks community are nearly all perennials with woody species predominant. The peculiar intermountain bristlecone pine occupies the exposed ridges where it is often dwarfed, misshapen, and extremely slow-growing. Interestingly, this species of tree represents the oldest living thing on earth. Pinyon pine and Utah juniper invade the breaks community from the foothills and valleys below the Paunsaugunt Plateau, whereas ponderosa pine, white fir, Douglas fir, blue spruce, and aspen trees occupy more favorable sites of the breaks. Associated plants in this community are the most hardy perennials, some woody and some herbaceous. A few annual plants invade each year but are sparse in distribution and poorly developed in growth.

ROCK COLUMBINE
Aquilegia scopulorum
Buttercup Family

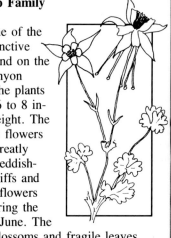

This is one of the most distinctive plants found on the Bryce Canyon breaks. The plants are only 6 to 8 inches in height. The vivid blue flowers contrast greatly with the reddish-colored cliffs and soil. The flowers bloom during the month of June. The delicate blossoms and fragile leaves seem out of place on the relatively barren slopes. The perennial rootstalks become thick and woody, persisting for many years on the steep, eroded slopes. The foliage of the plant is pale blue-green in color and rather sparse.

HEAD CRYPTANTHA, POPCORN
Cryptantha capitata   **Borage Family**

Clusters of tiny, white flowers with yellow centers terminate the branches of these diminutive plants. The blooming period is usually during the month of June. The foliage is bristly-hairy, with larger lance-shaped leaves at the base and smaller leaves up the stem. Most species of Cryptantha grow in dry soil, and several species are found on the dry, eroded slopes of the Bryce Canyon breaks and in the drier portions of forests above the canyon rim. Plants of this genus were used by Native Americans for treating boils.

BLUELEAF ASTER
Aster glaucodes
Sunflower Family

Whereas many wildflowers of the breaks community display vividly colored flowers and dark green foliage, the blueleaf aster appears faded in both herbage and bloom. August is the month for flower development. The leaves are whitish green in color and are elongated without petioles. The ray flowers of the flower heads are pale lavender or pink in color and surround a small cluster of yellow disk flowers. Numerous stems arise from creeping underground rhizomes, resulting in rather dense clumping of the plants wherever they occur. It is typical to see clusters of blueleaf asters along a trail of the breaks community. The blueleaf asters seem to harmonize in every respect with the colored slopes, cliffs, and pinnacles.

MAT PENSTEMON, DWARF BEARD-TONGUE

Penstemon caespitosus
Figwort Family

The stems of this penstemon are not over 2 inches tall, but are extremely numerous, forming dense mats up to 4 feet in diameter. The flowers are some of the smallest known of the penstemons, being only 1/2 to 3/4 of an inch long. The flowers are also very numerous and blend with the matted leaves to create an attractive natural ground cover. The mats are long-lived and are useful in combating soil erosion. Look for the flowers during midsummer.

CHAMBER TWINPOD   *Physaria chambersii*   **Mustard Family**

Flowers of plants belonging to the mustard family often have four petals and are in the shape of a crucifix. In early summer, the showy clusters of flowers of this plant are pale yellow. As flowers mature and develop into capsules, more flowers bloom so that a given plant may have unopened buds, fully developed flowers, and mature fruits at the same time. The leaves are elongated and spatula-shaped, numerous in the basal rosette but smaller and fewer on the stems. The leaves have many tiny branched hairs that give a silvery cast to the plant. The fruit eventually develops into a large, two-parted, inflated capsule, which is deeply notched at the apex. The genus Physaria is found only in western North America. The name *physaria* is Greek and means "bellows," which the inflated pod resembles.

HYMENOPAPPUS
Hymenopappus filifolius
Sunflower Family

This rather inconspicuous composite is typical of several members of the sunflower family in the Bryce Canyon breaks community. The stems bear a few heads, consisting of only tubular disk flowers that are bisexual and numerous. There are no showy ray flowers. Flowering is in mid-summer. The thick rootstalk branches to form clusters of finely dissected leaves with linear segments. It typically inhabits hills with poor soils.

THRIFTY GOLDENWEED
Haplopappus armeroides   **Sunflower Family**

This plant may be referred to as a subshrub inasmuch as it grows from a stout woody taproot and becomes somewhat mat-forming. The stems are rarely more than 2 to 6 inches tall, each bearing a single flower head in midsummer, consisting of bright orange ray flowers and dark brown disk flowers. The rigid and somewhat resinous leaves are erect and smooth-margined. The growth habitat is typically dry hills and slopes, which are often rocky ridges.

15

STEMLESS WOOLYBASE
Hymenoxys acaulis
Sunflower Family

This colorful, short plant grows on rocky hillsides. The flowering stalks are leafless and rise from a much-branched stout caudex, which is covered with hairy leaves. The flower heads are solitary and rather persistent. It is a bitter-tasting perennial and is reported to be poisonous to livestock, which rarely eat it. The Native Americans made a stimulating beverage from the plant and applied the leaves as a local anesthetic to alleviate pain.

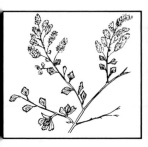

BUSH OCEAN SPRAY *Holodiscus dumosus* **Rose Family**

In the arid Southwest, these shrubs are of small scrubby form and are found on the steepest and rockiest of hillsides. The much-branched flower clusters develop in June, being somewhat feathery in appearance and creamy-white to pinkish in color. The foliage is aromatic with tiny leaf blades, which are densely white-silky underneath. The foliage is browsed by deer. The Native Americans used the small dry achenes for food. Some varieties of the plant have become popular for home planting.

RUBBER RABBITBRUSH *Chrysothamnus nauseosus* **Sunflower Family**

The generic name of this large shrub means "golden bush." The small yellow flowers are very numerous and cover the round-topped bushes with golden color in the late summer months. The stems are covered with a whitish and cotton-like material, and the leaves are linear in shape. This shrub invades disturbed areas, such as abused livestock ranges, roadsides, and eroded slopes. The abundance of the shrub on rangeland is an indication of overuse of the range by domestic livestock. The plant is probably avoided by animals because of its disagreeable rubbery taste. The common name refers to the presence of latex from which rubber can be made, but its extraction for commercial use is not profitable. Native Americans made a crude chewing gum from the plant, and also a yellow dye for their wool.

CURL-LEAF MOUNTAIN MAHOGANY

Cercocarpus ledifolius **Rose Family**

This rather large, dull-green shrub is typical of rocky outcrops on steep hillsides. It grows from 6 to 12 feet tall and is covered with stiff, leathery leaves, which are lance-shaped and have margins that curl under from the sides. The leaves are dark green on the upper surface and paler green to grayish beneath. June is the month for flower development of mountain mahoganies. The numerous pink blossoms are only 1/4 inch wide and have a texture of brushed felt. The fruits develop late in the summer as elongated structures attached to feathery spiraling plumes. The Native Americans of certain regions used the stems for digging and to make their bows and spears. The bark was used in a tea to cure colds. The shrub is excellent browse for deer.

ALDER-LEAF MOUNTAIN MAHOGANY

Cercocarpus montanus **Rose Family**

The alder-leaf mountain mahogany is an alpine shrub 3 to 10 feet in height that grows on dry ridges. The shrub has numerous stems that spread out from ground level. The shrub has leaves that are broad, slightly serrated, dark green and smooth above, and pale and sparsely hairy beneath. The bark is thin and grayish brown in color. The tiny pink blossoms are less than 1/2 inch wide and develop into fruits that are elongated and have spiral feathery tails. The shrubs often provide browse for deer and other forms of wildlife. The Native Americans gathered the thin bark, from which they made a red-brown dye.

ROCKY MOUNTAIN MAPLE

Acer glabrum   **Maple Family**

The Rocky Mountain maple appears as a well-formed shrub 5 to 10 feet tall or as a small tree with smooth, gray bark and slender branchlets. The leaves are variable in size but average 1 1/2 inches across and are smooth on both surfaces; deeply 3 to 5 lobed with margins unevenly toothed. The flowers are greenish yellow and develop into winged fruits for wind dispersal of seeds. The maple is found commonly in moist locations along streams, in canyons, and as undercover in forests on drier slopes. The leaves may be conspicuous due to red-colored insect galls. In the fall, the bright red leaf colors make a very showy display.

NATIONAL PARK SERVICE

UTAH SERVICEBERRY

Amelanchier utahensis **Rose Family**

Serviceberry is a slender shrub that has brown twigs with no thorns or prickles. The leaves are oval-shaped, slightly narrowed and finely toothed toward the tips. The flowers are produced in numerous short clusters in May or early June, and are fragrant, rose-like blossoms 1 inch in diameter. The berries mature in late summer and are dark blue or purple when ripe. Although the fruit is seedy and bland, it was an important food for both the Native Americans and pioneers. Europeans made pies and puddings from the berries, always leaving the seeds in, as they added to the flavor. The Native Americans also used the fresh berries for soups or dried them and pounded them up with dried meat or animal fat for use on long trips. Such a mixture was called ''pemmican.'' In addition, the Native Americans used the wood for arrow shafts.

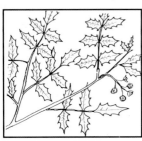

FREMONT BARBERRY

Mahonia fremontii   **Barberry Family**

The pale green fremont barberry has evergreen leaves that are compound and has spiny-tipped leaflets, which are thick and leathery. The six-parted yellow flowers are arranged into short, loose clusters. The berries, which develop from the flowers, are dark blue, dry, and inflated at maturity. The shrubs often grow on steep, dry slopes. The Native Americans used the root for a tonic and made a yellow dye from the plant for buckskins, cloth, and baskets. They also made various articles and tools from the wood. The plants are somewhat poisonous to livestock, but are browsed by deer when other food is scarce. The plant is not used in landscaping because it may be a secondary host of blackstem rust of cereal grain.

TWO-NEEDLE PINYON
Pinus edulis   **Pine Family**

This is a low, picturesque tree, 12 to 30 feet tall, with fissured bark. The trunk and branches of the tree are often crooked. The needles are stiff, incurved, and gray-green in color, two to a bundle. The cones are light-brown, approximately 2 inches long and 2 inches in diameter, bearing large, tasty seeds. The pinyon grows where other pines cannot grow, in semiarid areas that have hot summers and often slightly alkaline soils. It is one of the smallest of the pines and has very slow growth. It grows in association with Utah juniper to compose the pinyon-juniper woodland, sometimes called the "pygmy forest," which is so extensive in the southwestern United States. The pinyon seeds or nuts have long been a staple food for the Native Americans. The harvest is extremely variable from one year to the next. The large edible pine nuts rank in commercial value second to the pecan among the wild nut trees of the United States.

UTAH JUNIPER

Juniperus osteosperma   **Cypress Family**

Coarse, scale-like leaves characterize this rather dense, rounded, pygmy forest tree, which is 8 to 15 feet tall at maturity. The female cones are berry-like with only the scale tips projecting from the smooth, bluish brown surface at maturity. There are usually 1 to 5 seeds per cone and the seeds are wingless. The trees grow in the most arid conditions of the Southwest, often on hillsides where soil is somewhat alkaline, but with good drainage. The wood is very durable and is commonly used for fence posts. The berry-like cones are eaten by birds and small mammals, but the seeds are indigestible, being eliminated by the bird or animal as waste. The process of passing through the animal digestive tract softens the seedcoats, breaking dormancy and allowing germination.

BRISTLECONE PINE

Pinus longaeva   **Pine Family**

The growth habit of the bristlecone pine is variable, dependent upon environmental conditions of the habitat. It often has a dense, bushy crown with dark green needles, which are clustered along a branch to resemble a fox's tail. The needles are in bundles of 5, stout and curved, and long-persistent, to 1 1/2 inches long. The female cones are purplish brown; the scales are thickened and ridged with fragile, bristle-like incurved prickles. The trees are very slow-growing on exposed areas on dry, rocky soils where they are often stunted and misshapen by harsh growing conditions. They often reach great longevity at high elevations. Bryce Canyon breaks is the lowest elevation in the distribution of the bristlecone pine. Representatives of this species may be seen along the Queens Garden Trail. The trees can be found growing almost to the timberline in southern Utah, such as at Cedar Breaks.

Ponderosa Pine Forests of Bryce Canyon

I n striking contrast to the extreme slope conditions of the breaks at Bryce Canyon is the moderate topography of the ponderosa pine forest, which extends westward from the canyon rim at elevations less than 8,500 feet. This area is truly the top of the plateau, having only slight to moderate slopes.

The forest occupying the northern portion of the Paunsaugunt Plateau within Bryce Canyon National Park has ponderosa pine as an overwhelmingly dominant species. Other kinds of trees in this forest occupy only minor roles, being much smaller and fewer in number than the abundant and massive ponderosa pine.

The forest is characteristically open, with trees spaced well apart, providing space, sunlight, adequate soil moisture, and nutrients for growth of shrubs such as manzanita, bitterbrush, and mountain lilac. Grasses and conspicuous flowering plants are abundant among the shrubs, especially where soil is well-developed. Because the forest canopy is seldom dense and continuous over an extensive area, most of these herbaceous plants are sun-loving species and thrive in the forest understory.

Grazing of the area by domestic animals for fifty years prior to the establishment of Bryce Canyon National Park in 1928 caused considerable accelerated erosion. The northern portion of Bryce Canyon National Park was fenced in 1935, but recovery of the vegetation and the soil has been slow. Evidences of continued rapid erosion are: the presence of pedestaled plants with the root crown well above the general soil level, rills on hillsides, and small rock particles left behind on the soil surface after sheet erosion has removed the finer soil materials. A tree that happens to fall at a right angle to the direction of the slope forms a dam, above which eroding soil is eventually deposited almost to the depth of the diameter of the log.

The height of the broad-leafed evergreen shrubs in this forest is an indication of the depth of the snow during the winters of least snowfall. Such evergreen shrubs are severely damaged or killed by the subzero temperatures of midwinter unless the snow protects them. The temperature below the surface of a snowbank does not get lower than freezing temperature; therefore, snow is an excellent layer of insulation for shrubs and protects them from frost burn.

YARROW
Achillea millefolium
Sunflower Family

Western yarrow is a perennial herb with a strong but pleasant odor. The numerous leaves are pinnately dissected into 5 divisions and have a fernlike appearance. The flower heads develop in mid-summer and are composed of numerous, minute, white flowers in flat-topped clusters. The flower heads are tiny within floral sprays that vary from 3 to 6 inches in diameter. The Native Americans had many medicinal uses for the plant. The whole plant was picked and dried. The leaves were used to stop bleeding of wounds and to heal inflammation. A handful of the plant boiled in water was a tonic or tea for indigestion, toothache, or for general run-down conditions of health. When the plant is eaten by cattle it imparts a disagreeable flavor to milk; however, neither cattle nor sheep utilize it unless forced to do so on overgrazed ranges.

CB

PACIFIC ASTER   *Aster adscendens*   **Sunflower Family**

Asters are attractive summer- or fall-flowering herbs that usually grow from spreading or much-branched rootstalks. The heads are usually numerous in clusters, each with approximately 25 lavender ray flowers encircling the yellow disk flowers. The name *Aster* is Greek, meaning "star," and describes the radiate heads of the flowers. The stems have numerous, small, lance-shaped leaves. Asters commonly inhabit dry, rocky hillsides. They are often confused with fleabanes (*Erigeron*), which have many very narrow ray flowers (30 to 150). Fleabanes usually bloom in spring and early summer instead of the last part of the growing season.

NARROW LEAF OR WYOMING PAINTBRUSH
Castilleja linariifolia   **Figwort Family**

The narrowleaf or Wyoming paintbrush is taller than most other species of Indian paintbrush and has leaves that are narrow and grasslike, being divided into narrow segments. When in bloom in July, the plants have impressive, bright red flowers. Actually, the real flowers of the plant are inconspicuous and small but are surrounded by bracts and upper leaves that are highly colored. The flowers are tubular and green-tipped, and occur in dense clusters at the end of branches, with red or scarlet leaflike bracts below each of them. The plant is a semiparasite, producing only part of the food it requires. Its roots grow into the soil until they touch roots of other plants, such as sagebrush. The roots penetrate the tissues of the host plant to take part of their food.

LIMESTONE THISTLE
Cirsium calcareum   **Sunflower Family**

This thistle is a common, attractive roadside flower. It has a long blooming season, from June until October. It often occurs on rocky slopes in open spaces among trees, where it grows 2 to 3 feet tall. The thistles are noted for sharp prickles that stick out from the leaves and stems. Such "armed" plants are protected from grazing cattle. The vivid purple disk flowers are tightly clustered in heads, which are grouped to give a striking mass effect. The heads face upward to the sun and are often visited by hummingbirds. Native Americans dug up and ate the fleshy roots of this thistle.

REDROOT BUCKWHEAT
Eriogonum racemosum
Buckwheat Family

The redroot buckwheat has slender, leafless, flowering stems, which branch to bear dense clusters of small, white or pink flowers. The rootstalk is woody, few-branched, and bears oblong basal leaves, which are smooth, pale green above and covered with fine, dense hairs underneath. The name *Eriogonum* comes from Greek, meaning "woolly joints." The seeds of this plant are gathered by chipmunks and white-footed mice.

WESTERN WALLFLOWER
Erysimum asperum   **Mustard Family**

The western wallflower is a very attractive wildflower that blooms in late June or early July. In Europe, plants of this genus often grow against old walls, hence the name. The bright yellow flowers are composed of four petals, sometimes tinged with orange. The elongated flower cluster is dense with individual flowers about 1/2 inch in diameter. The leaves are narrow, and both leaves and stems have microscopic pick-shaped hairs that are attached at the middle. The pods that develop from the flowers are elongate and slender structures. The plants of the mustard family have a watery and pungent juice, containing a glycoside that hydrolyzes to oil of mustard. CB

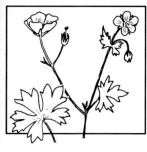

SMALL-LEAF GERANIUM
Geranium caespitosum   **Geranium Family**

The wild geraniums are herbs that have forked stems that are swollen at the points where leaves are attached. They are reminiscent of domestic geraniums, and belong to the same family. The small-leaf geranium is rather diminutive and sparsely branched as it is found in the mountains of southern Utah. The dark green leaves are deeply lobed and finely toothed. The rose-pink, veined flowers appear in midsummer and eventually form into beaked structures resembling cranes' bills. These beaked structures split from the bottom upward when fully ripe, and scatter the seeds over a wide area.

SCARLET GILIA, SKYROCKET
Gilia aggregata
Phlox Family

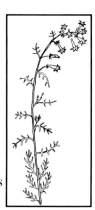

The scarlet gilia or skyrocket is one of the showiest of wildflowers. The plants are biennial, with the flowering stem elongating during the second season from a basal rosette of leaves. The slender flowers are borne in loose clusters on sparsely leafed stems and are from 1 to 1 1/2 inches long. The star-shaped tubular flowers are commonly red, but some forms of the plant have pink, orange, or white flowers. Hummingbirds and moths are attracted to the flowers and help in the cross-pollinating process. The plants have a heavy, slightly skunklike odor.

KENTROPHYTA
Astragalus kentrophyta   **Legume Family**

The kentrophyta is an attractive natural groundcover wherever it occurs. It often covers areas several feet in diameter with low, matted stems bearing numerous gray-green, compound, spiny-tipped leaves. The miniature, pea-shaped flowers are purple in color. The plant is typically found in open, timbered areas where it fills the valuable role of prevention of soil erosion. The tiny, colorful flowers make a striking contrast to the silvery-green foliage.

THORN WIRELETTUCE
Stephanomeria spinosa
Sunflower Family

The lower leaves of the thorn wirelettuce plant are elongated and stiff. On the upper portion of the stems the leaves are reduced to scales, and above each scale-like leaf, a long spine projects outward from the pale green stem. The stems often have many rigid zigzag branchlets. The flowering period is midsummer. The flower heads are very small and are composed of merely 3 to 5 delicate pink ray flowers. The plants thrive in dry, sandy or rocky soil.

J. L. CRAWFORD

SOUTHWESTERN STONESEED

Lithospermum multiflorum   **Borage Family**

Numerous tiny, orange-yellow flowers cover the rather large
and bushy plants of Southwestern stoneseed during the month
of June. The edges of the corolla lobes have smooth margins.
The leaves are long, narrow, and somewhat hairy. At the base
of each of the stems, a vivid purple pigment may be seen. The
purple pigment is very heavily concentrated in the roots of the
plant and was extracted by Native Americans for coloring
garments and feathers. The seeds of the plant are hard, white,
and shiny. The name *Lithospermum* means ''stone-seed.''

SHOWY STONESEED
Lithospermum incisum
Borage Family

In contrast to the Southwestern stoneseed, the showy stoneseed has relatively few stems and larger flowers. The slender, yellow corolla tubes have five lobes, which have toothed, scalloped, or cut edges. The stoneseeds grow well in dry, stony soil and have a long midsummer blooming period. The seeds are very hard. Roots of this plant were often used by Native Americans for medicine or food.

CURLYCUP GUMWEED
Grindelia squarrosa   **Sunflower Family**

Among the first plants to invade disturbed areas, such as roadsides, is the ragged-looking and multi-branched curlycup gumweed with its numerous yellow flowers. The leaves and flower buds are covered with a clear, sticky substance. The leaves are numerous and more or less toothed. Curlycup gumweed typically blooms from July to September and adds much color to otherwise drab disturbed sites. Native Americans used curlycup gumweed for medicine, for chewing, and as a substitute for tea. The plant has been used to provide relief of poison ivy miseries.

SHOWY RUSH PINK
Lygodesmia grandiflora
Sunflower Family

One of the very attractive plants of the ponderosa pine forest is the showy rush pink. The head of ray flowers superficially resembles some members of the pink family whereas the sparsely to moderately branched plant with grass-like leaves resembles rush plants. Actually, the showy rush pink is not related to either the pinks nor the rushes, but is a composite, having stems and leaves that exude a milky juice when cut or bruised, as does dandelion and many other composites. The pink-colored flower heads consist only of ray flowers, develop in July, and are unusually large for such a sparse plant. The plant thrives in dry, open places in the forest. Native Americans boiled the leaves of the plant with meat to improve the flavor.

BRONZE EVENING PRIMROSE
Oenothera howardii
Evening Primrose Family

A candidate for the most strikingly beautiful wildflower at Bryce Canyon is certainly the large-flowered bronze evening primrose. To enjoy this flower at its best, one must look for it early in the morning because the blossoms soon fade in the heat of the day to a reddish cluster. The individual flowers appear, like theatrical stars on tour, "for one night only." New buds open farther along the spike on succeeding evenings, however. The leaves are tufted, thick in texture, lance-shaped in outline, and shiny dark green in color. The plant grows in dry places, often on limestone soils, which are so common near the rim of Bryce Canyon. The floral display is especially vivid during summers following wet winter and spring seasons, but a few of the hardy plants bloom even during summers of drought.

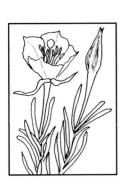

LAVENDER EVENING PRIMROSE
Calyophus lavandulifolius   **Evening Primrose Family**

The flowers of evening primroses have extremely long corollas with the stigma and nectaries deep inside the tube. The flowers bloom at night and are pollinated mainly by moths, which have long tubular mouthparts for use in obtaining the nectar from the flowers. The lavender evening primrose flower remains in bloom throughout the day, persisting longer during daylight hours than the larger showy evening primrose. The plant is multi-branched and covered with rather small leaves. The floral tubes are capped with four scalloped lobes that are delicate in form and color. The plants are numerous throughout the ponderosa pine forests of Bryce Canyon.

BLACK GROUNDSEL
Senecio atratus **Sunflower Family**

An attractive roadside flower at both Bryce Canyon and Cedar Breaks is the black groundsel with its pale bluish green, spatula-shaped leaves and clusters of many tiny flower heads. The tiny ray flowers are light yellow in color. The generic name *Senecio* means "old man," in reference to the white hairy attachments to the tiny dry fruits as the flower heads mature. The plants prefer dry, often rocky, soil on mountain slopes through several forest zones up to timberline. CB

BROOM GROUNDSEL *Senecio spartioides* **Sunflower Family**

These fairly large bushy plants are very conspicuous at Bryce Canyon throughout the summer along roadsides, on dry, stony slopes, and on edges of meadows. Many stems develop from a heavy, woody rootstalk. The stems are heavy all the way to the clusters of heads that terminate every stem. The leaves are many, linear in shape, and have smooth margins. The heads are upright, each containing only a few ray flowers. The plant is known to be poisonous to livestock, but is rarely eaten by them.

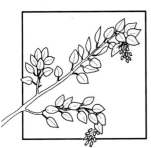

GREENLEAF MANZANITA

Arctostaphylos patula **Heather Family**

The bright green leaves and smooth, mahogany-red bark on crooked, spreading branches make this an attractive shrub. It often grows in thickets among the large ponderosa pine trees. In early summer there are clusters of nodding, pink, urn-shaped flowers, which later develop into green, berry-like fruits having a soft pulp surrounding several seeds. Manzanita is Spanish, meaning "little apple." Chipmunks, squirrels, and birds eat the berries at Bryce Canyon. The plant is evergreen and survives the cold winters in the high mountains under an insulating cover of snow. The Native Americans ate the berries raw, cooked, or ground into a meal. The fruits and leaves have astringent properties and were crushed for treating bronchitis and the inflammation caused by poison ivy.

BITTERBRUSH *Purshia tridentata* **Rose Family**

Bitterbrush is an intricately branched shrub 2 to 3 feet tall at Bryce Canyon with grayish green, aromatic foliage. The leaves are small, thick, and leathery. They are wedge-shaped and 3-toothed at the tip, white-felty below, and with the side margins somewhat inrolled. The shrubs spread out laterally. The numerous, yellow blossoms have five petals and are borne on short branchlets. The dry, hard, bitter fruits are narrowed to a slender tip and taper to the base. Rodents relish the bitter fruit. The shrubs commonly occur on dry, south-facing slopes where they provide browse for deer, even though the foliage is very bitter. Native Americans made medicine from the bark for treating eye infections and a decoction, or boiled-down concentrate from the leaves, was used as a cough syrup.

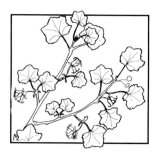

WAX CURRANT *Ribes cereum* **Saxifrage Family**

The wax currant is a rigid, very intricately-branched shrub 1 to 6 feet high, with musky, scented herbage. The leaves are somewhat round in outline, slightly 3 to 5 lobed with finely toothed margins, and dull green color. The young leaves are glandular and sticky to the touch. The flowers are pinkish and develop into bright red, smooth berries that are glandular-dotted. The berries are edible, but are rather insipid or nauseating. Deer browse the twigs considerably, especially at Bryce Canyon, and the berries are eaten by many birds and mammals. The currants lack the characteristic prickles of their close relative, the prickly currant.

MOUNTAIN SNOWBERRY

Symphoricarpos oreophilus   **Honeysuckle Family**

The spreading shrubs, 1 to 3 feet high, have thin, rounded leaves that are smooth and light bluish-green in color. The flowers grow in terminal clusters and have floral tubes that are bell-shaped and pale pink in color. Late in summer, the blossoms are replaced by clusters of waxy white berries that contain two very hard seeds. The fruits are unpalatable for human consumption, but are a valuable food source for birds and small mammals. The shrubs often form dense stands on wooded hillsides, where they serve as protective cover for birds. Native Americans made a decoction for colds and stomachache by pounding and steeping the roots. The leaves contain saponin, a poisonous drug. The shrub is often used as an ornamental plant in landscaping.

UTAH MOUNTAIN LILAC
Ceanothus martinii **Buckthorn Family**

These shrubs are low, open, and rigidly branched without spines. The leaves are small, oval, smooth, green on both surfaces, and with three prominent veins from the base. The flowers are very tiny and white and are borne in dense clusters. The branches and twigs are grayish in color. The shrub provides important browse for deer and other forms of wildlife.

CHOKECHERRY *Prunus virginiana* **Rose Family**

The chokecherry becomes a tall shrub or small tree with smooth, reddish brown bark. The leaves are shiny and attractive, but are poisonous to some browsing animals in early spring. The blossoms are white and are borne in long clusters that resemble bottle-brushes. The green, cherry-like fruits of early summer gradually turn red, then become black at maturity. The raw fruits have a bitter, astringent flavor, but are relished by birds and small mammals. The shrubs grow in shaded sites, moist hillsides, and in valleys, sometimes forming dense thickets. The berries are useful to man when prepared as a jelly combined with apples or other fruits.

ROCKY MOUNTAIN JUNIPER

Juniperus scopulorum　**Cypress Family**

The Rocky Mountain juniper is a rather small- to medium-sized tree of the ponderosa pine forest belt, growing along streams and usually on north-facing slopes of canyons. The dark green leaves and blue, berry-like cones are covered with a white, powdery bloom. The juvenile leaves are needle-like, but the older leaves are small and scale-like. The reddish brown bark grows in narrow ridges and is sometimes fibrous and shreddy. The wood is reddish in color and is durable but, because of the crookedness and mostly small size of the trunks, is of little value as lumber. Its chief use is as fence posts. The seeds are widely disseminated since the cones are readily eaten by many mammals and birds. The seeds are not digested, and their passage through the digestive tract of the mammal or bird prepares the seeds for ger-mination when released with digestive wastes, often far from the site of the tree that produced the cones. Some varieties of the tree are popularly used in landscaping.

PONDEROSA PINE

Pinus ponderosa **Pine Family**

This large, dominant forest tree has a pyramidal crown when young, often becoming flat-topped with age. It occurs in open, park-like stands on dry, well-drained, exposed, southerly slopes or plateaus. The leaves are in bundles of 3 or sometimes 2 and attain lengths of 5 to 10 inches. The cones are approximately 3 inches in length with prickles that curve outwardly on the cone scales. The bark on older trees is thick, deeply furrowed, reddish brown in color, and divided into large plates that scale off. The odor of the bark is resinous. The gummy pitch from the bark is very adhesive and was used by Native Americans for canoes and tents. The seeds have a pleasant taste, which may be crushed or ground and then made into a bread with the addition of sunflower seeds. The dwarf mistletoe that grows on this pine was used by Native Americans in a decoction as a stomach aid and to relieve colic.

LIMBER PINE

Pinus flexilis   **Pine Family**

The limber pine is a handsome, dark green, round-topped tree, which is commonly found in our forests from Bryce Canyon rim upward to timberline in southern Utah. The bark is gray or silvery white when the tree is young and becomes dark brown to grayish in older trees. It forms somewhat rectangular scaly plates between the furrows of old tree trunks. The leaves are in bundles of five and grow as tufts at the ends of branches. The trees thrive on dry sunny slopes. Near timberline on mountains, the trees are reduced in size to shrubs, which are greatly misshapen by ice-borne winter winds and very cold temperatures.

High Plateau Sagebrush Communities

The lowest depressions on top of the Paunsaugunt Plateau and near Bryce Canyon National Park are not forested. The ponderosa pine forests end abruptly some distance away from the intermittent stream channels that thread their way westward toward the East Fork of the Sevier River. Occupying the relatively flat depression in these broad valleys is the sagebrush community. The dominant shrub is the small black sage. Various other small shrubs and subshrubs are associated with the black sage, such as Southwest rabbitbrush, Colorado rubberweed, matchbrush, and gray horsebrush. Short bunch grasses and broad-leafted flowering plants may be found associated with the various shrubs.

The boundary between the well developed sagebrush community and the ponderosa pine forests is interesting. Young ponderosa pine trees and Rocky Mountain juniper trees may be found ''invading'' the sagebrush flats, but they do not survive long enough to establish a mature forest for replacement of the brushland. The forest cannot become established in these depressions because of severe winter minimum temperatures caused by cold air drainage from higher mountain areas. The cold air settles in these lowest depressions, pushing the warmer air upward, thus creating a thermal inversion. Daily temperature fluctuations in these lowest depressions are tremendous and minimum temperature differences between the sagebrush flats and the pine forests may be as great as 30° F. On a typical January night, the forest minimum temperature may be 0° F, at the same time as the sagebrush community has a minimum temperature of minus 30° F.

The soils of the sagebrush flats are generally deeper than those of the surrounding forested slopes due to alluvial transport of material by running water. Considerable topsoil has been lost from this community during and following the fifty-year period of heavy over-grazing by domestic livestock. Erosion check dams were installed in the mid-1930s and have helped control gully development along the intermittent stream channels. The amount of sediment collected behind check dams is indicative of the continued high level of sheet erosion that is taking place.

Plant diversity is great in the sagebrush community. Many colorful wildflowers and grasses may be found here. There are a number of dry meadows occupying the very lowest depressions. In springtime, there is abundant moisture here to support the shrubby cinquefoil, parry bellflower, wild iris, and shooting star, in addition to thick stands of sedges and grasses.

BLUE FLAX
Linum lewisii   **Flax Family**

The flowers of the blue flax are borne on very slender and slightly nodding stems. These flowers are very fragile, often losing the petals soon after opening to full bloom. The stems are slender and sway in the slightest breeze. Several stems arise from a branched rootstalk and contain long, tough fibers. Many slender, pointed leaves are borne along the stems. The flowers, which develop in midsummer, vary from deep blue to pale blue to white. Native Americans had many uses for the plants: the seeds were cooked with other foods to add flavor and nutrition; the stems and leaves were steeped for treatment of stomach disorders, eye infections, and swelling; the fibers were used for cords and fish lines. When eaten by livestock, the blue flax causes drowsiness. Cultivated flax is another species of the same genus, and provides us with fibers and linseed oil.

KING FLAX
Linum kingii   **Flax Family**

The king flax is considerably shorter in height than the blue flax. The cluster of delicate yellow flowers is narrow and crowded near the tip of the stem. Numerous stems with many short, narrow, shiny leaves typify this flax. It is easy to recognize this plant even when the flowers are not present. The petals of the flowers are smaller than those of the blue flax, but are equally fragile and ephemeral. The king flax grows only at high elevations in mountains.

COLORADO RUBBER PLANT

Hymenoxys richardsonii
Sunflower Family

This many-branched plant from a woody crown grows to a height of 6 to 18 inches. The many flower heads bloom at the same time, giving the plant a flat-topped appearance. Both the disk and ray flowers are bright yellow in color and the leaves are greatly elongated. The plants are toxic to livestock, especially sheep, but are not eaten until other forage is very scarce. These plants tend to increase on overgrazed ranges. The plants produce a latex that contains rubber, but it is economically unfeasible to extract it commercially. The bark of the root was used as a substitute for chewing gum by Native Americans.

MISSOURI IRIS
Iris missouriensis **Iris Family**

The beautiful Missouri iris may be found in grassy meadows in the lowest parts of the open areas at Bryce Canyon, where soil moisture is most abundant. It is not found on the sur- rounding sagebrush flats. The variegated violet-blue flowers are delicate replicas of the cultivated iris. Several flowers are borne on stems that are 1 to 2 feet tall. The leaves are narrow and sword-like. The plants rise from rhizomes, which may spread to form clumps or solid stands in meadows. The leaves and rhizomes are poisonous to livestock, due to the presence of irisin, which is a violent emetic and cathartic. CB

WHITE TUFTED EVENING PRIMROSE
Oenothera caespitosa **Evening Primrose Family**

This is a strikingly beautiful wildflower, which is known for conspicuous, fragrant, white flowers 3 to 4 inches in diameter. The corolla tubes are 2 to 3 inches long and rise from a tuft of narrow leaves. The four petals are lobed and turn pink to red as they mature. The toothed leaves are 2 to 6 inches long and are clustered about a woody root crown. Stems are absent, although the elongated corolla tube may resemble a stem. Flowers open at night and are pollinated by moths. The flowers remain open during the day, in con- trast to the bronze evening primrose, which has a yellow flower that wilts during mid- morning.

SHRUBBY CINQUEFOIL
Potentilla fruticosa   **Rose Family**

The shrubby cinquefoil is a very attractive, many-branched shrub 1 to 3 feet tall at Bryce Canyon, with bright yellow flowers, which are about 3/4 inches broad. The shrubs typically grow in rocky, subalpine meadows near timberline, but are found in the low depressions at Bryce Canyon where moisture is most abundant, especially from snowmelt and spring run-off. The leaves are divided with the leaflets narrow in outline. The flowers superficially resemble buttercups. Deer and domestic livestock eat the foliage, which has a rather coarse texture and astringent taste. Stockmen and wildlife biologists use this plant as one of the indicators in determining range conditions and trends.

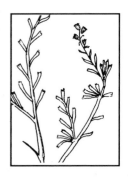

BLACK SAGEBRUSH *Artemisia nova* **Sunflower Family**

The black sagebrush is a low, spreading, evergreen shrub with light to dark brown bark. It is found on dry, rocky places at Bryce Canyon where winter minimum temperatures are too low to permit forest growth, such as the lowest parts of shallow valleys on the Paunsaugunt Plateau. The leaves are silvery-white due to dense, fine hairs that cover leaf surfaces. The flowers are in erect, spike-like clusters and are extremely tiny. The shrubs are browsed somewhat by deer. Due to excessive erosion from past overgrazing, present use of wildlife, and adversities of winter climatic conditions, the shrubs are kept stunted and misshapen.

DWARF RABBITBRUSH *Chrysothamnus depressus* **Sunflower Family**

This relatively small rabbitbrush has smooth branches bearing alternate leaves, which are narrowly linear and smooth on both surfaces. The flower heads are small and contain only disk flowers, which are yellow in color. Each individual flower head bears only 5 disk flowers, but the heads are very numerous at the ends of the stems. None of the species of rabbitbrush have forage value, and therefore tend to increase on overgrazed and over-browsed ranges as the more palatable plants are over-used and destroyed. The Native Americans obtained a yellow dye from the flowers and a green dye from the inner bark of the rabbitbrush.

GRAY HORSEBRUSH

Tetradymia canescens   **Sunflower Family**

The gray horsebrush is an intricately-branched shrub varying from 1 to 2 feet in height. It has grayish branches and leaves, due to numerous, tiny hairs on the surfaces. The leaves are narrowly linear and straight. The flower heads are light yellow in color and are clustered along the many-branched stems. These shrubs inhabit dry, open places in foothills and forest openings. Horsebrush stands up under—and often above—the snow, and is often eaten by wild and domestic animals when other food is scarce. The plant may be responsible for causing bighead malady in domestic sheep. The plants are most toxic in spring during their early growth. On poor ranges, they are eaten by sheep that are being trailed to shearing corrals and summer ranges.

PARRY BELLFLOWER

Campanula parryi   **Bellflower Family**

This attractive bellflower inhabits moist, subalpine meadows
and the moist areas among sagebrush. It is a perennial plant
from branching, slender rootstalks. The leaves are smooth and
shiny, and have smooth margins. The basal leaves are elliptic
in outline. The flowers are typically solitary with blue to purple
corolla tubes, which are broadly bell-shaped with five lobes.
The stems are rather slender, and the flowers are erect or
slightly nodding.

LONGLEAF PHLOX   *Phlox longifolia*   **Phlox Family**

The handsome longleaf phlox frequently occurs in compact, tufted mats of foliage and flowers in early June. The stems may be solitary, but often spread by means of creeping rhizomes to form patches of woody stems below the herbaceous stems, which bear the leaves and flowers. The leaves are lance-shaped, gray-green in color, soft to the touch, lightly hairy, and from 1 to 2 inches long. The corolla of the flower consists of 5 united petals, which are pink to lavender or white and often reach a diameter of 1/2 inch. This phlox is widespread in distribution in Utah, occurring in every county of the state as well as in surrounding states. It is found in many different habitats also, but at Bryce Canyon is most often seen in sagebrush communities.

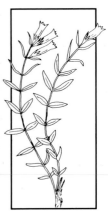

PARRY GENTIAN   *Gentiana parryi*   **Gentian Family**

The Parry gentian is often hard to find among the shrubs and grasses of the open flats at Bryce Canyon. It favors the lowest depressions where soil mosture is retained the longest as the growing season progresses. Several stems usually spread out from the base of a plant and then ascend upward to bear leaves in pairs. The flowers are closely crowded toward the ends of the stems. The calyx, or lowest outer flower part, is a funnel-shaped green tube tinged with purple, having unequal pointed lobes. The corolla is a narrow tube of deep blue color, often mottled or streaked with green. There are five sharp-pointed lobes to the corolla.

Fir-Spruce-Aspen Forests

 rather dense forest of mixed conifers and aspen occupies the southern portion of the Paunsaugunt Plateau within and adjacent to Bryce Canyon National Park. The slopes of the top of the plateau are generally moderate, but several westward-running drainages are very steep and forested. A comparable forest occurs at the foot of the steep cliffs of Cedar Breaks National Monument but is inaccessible to visitors. The fir-spruce-aspen forests may be seen along the roads leading to Cedar Breaks at lower elevations on the Markagunt Plateau.

White fir and Douglas fir are abundant on all except the driest of slopes. Ponderosa pine and Rocky Mountain juniper are often found on south- and west-facing rocky outcrops, which are warmer and drier due to poor soils and to the more direct angle of the sun's rays. Blue spruce trees generally occupy the bottoms of ravines, where soil moisture is most abundant.

In forest succession conifer trees slowly replace aspen trees. The aspen are the first trees to invade an area from which the conifer forests may have been removed, such as following a fire. With long-continued succession in the absence of fire, the aspen trees at Bryce Canyon are disappearing. There are a few well-developed aspen groves left, and the bright aspen foliage offers an interesting contrast to the dark green color of the evergreen forest, especially during the fall season when the aspen leaves turn golden.

Under the dense conifer stands grow few shrubs or herbaceous plants due to low light intensities and thick forest litter. Common juniper, snowberry, wild rose, and mountain lover persist due to possession of a degree of shade tolerance. Wildflowers are generally scarce in these conifer groves. Aspen groves are more open than are conifer stands, and permit enough light to reach the forest floor so that many flowering plants can thrive and bloom. These flower gardens spread from aspen groves into openings among the dense conifer stands. Along the highway to Rainbow Point within Bryce Canyon National Park, the arrowleaf balsamroot and other colorful wildflowers present a display during the blooming season.

ARROWLEAF BALSAMROOT   *Balsamorhiza sagittata*   **Sunflower Family**

Several stems arise from a dense, perennial rootstalk bearing large, yellow flower heads in early summer. The leaf blades are shaped like elongated, inverted hearts and are attached to long petioles. The herbage is pale silvery-green, due to the presence of numerous minute hairs on the surface. Arrowleaf balsamroot occurs on dry hills and in dry forest openings. The large root can be used for food after several washings and cookings to remove the bitter taste. Native Americans obtained a medicine from boiling the roots for treatment of rheumatism or headache. The patient was covered following treatment as the drug caused profuse perspiration. Native Americans also cracked and ground the seeds into a meal, which was made into a gruel for food. Gum from the root was collected for chewing.

SHOWY GOLDENEYE
Heliomeris multiflora
Sunflower Family

The roadside to Rainbow Point in Bryce Canyon National Park is decorated in late summer with patches of showy goldeneye. A slender, branching plant with dark green leaves, it is covered with very many medium-sized flower heads that resemble sunflowers. Both the ray and disk flowers are yellow in color. The leaves are narrowly lance-shaped and slightly toothed. Roadsides, dry slopes, and openings in the forest are ideal places to find this attractive wildflower. CB

ROCK GOLDENROD

Petradoria pumila
Sunflower Family

The rock goldenrod was once considered in the same genus with the goldenrods. It could be considered a subshrub, having a woody rootstalk and stem base, but all of the new growth is herbaceous each year. The leaves are long and narrow, and very rigid due to the presence of silica compounds. The typical habitat of the rock goldenrod is thin, rocky, dry soils. It blooms in late summer with numerous small, yellow heads in clusters.

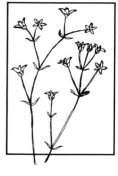

FENDLER SANDWORT   *Arenaria fendleri*   **Pink Family**

Sandworts have narrow stems and pointed leaves. The leaves lack petioles and the base of the slender leafblade clasps the stem. The numerous stems of the fendler sandwort bear tufts of sharp leaves and tiny, white blossoms. Each tiny flower has five white petals that provide a backdrop for the 10 red anthers to show up as dark spots. The clusters of plants often form cushions or mats that carpet and protect the soil from erosion for many years. The fendler sandwort is often associated with limestone rock formations, which are prevalent in the Bryce Canyon area.

MOUNTAIN LOVER
Paxistima myrsinites   **Staff-Tree Family**

Normally a low-spreading, many-branched woody shrub that often occurs in dense patches on the forest floor, the mountain lover at Bryce Canyon is so seriously overbrowsed that only little sprigs of new growth at ground level may be found due to the frequent harvest by deer. The plants have small, dark green, thick evergreen leaves, which are slightly toothed and resemble the boxwood of ornamental gardens. The clusters of dark red blossoms are very small and are borne in leaf axils. The mountain lover is one of the most attractive small shrubs of the forest because of its shiny, dark green foliage.

OREGON GRAPE

Mahonia repens   **Barberry Family**

This species of Oregon grape is a close relative of the state flower of Oregon, but differs in that it is a prostrate ground cover instead of a shrub. The leaves are shiny, leathery, and evergreen, with spiny teeth along the margins, resembling the leaves of holly. The leaves turn bright red in the fall of the year. The bright yellow flowers of May and June grow in clusters, which develop into dark, bluish-purple berries that resemble grapes. The berries are very acrid to the taste. The fruit was used for food by the Native Americans, who also made a yellow dye from the woody stems. They dried roots of the plant for treatment of ulcers and sores. The stems are usually greatly elongated under the soil surface, and new plants arise along this underground stem, forming dense groundcover.

CB

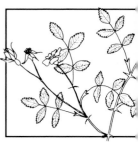

NOOTKA ROSE *Rosa nutkana* **Rose Family**

The nootka rose occurs along intermittent streams in open woods. It is mostly a low shrub with stems "armed" with straight or somewhat curved, slender prickles. The leaves are compound with 5 to 7 leaflets. The flowers are about 1 inch in diameter and vary in color from pale pink to deep rose. The fruit is a globose hip, which is nutritious food, containing massive doses of vitamin C. The fresh fruits may be cooked or slightly dried fruits may be ground up and used as a meal or flour. Rose plants are an important browse species. The relatively few wild rose plants left at Bryce Canyon are in poor condition from past heavy use by deer. CB

BLUE ELDERBERRY *Sambucus cerulea* **Honeysuckle Family**

A characteristic large shrub of the montane forests of southern Utah is the blue elderberry. It normally has several main stems from the base, which are jointed and hollow. The leaves are smooth and divided into a number of leaflets. The clusters of numerous, tiny, white or cream-colored flowers are flat-topped and lacy in appearance. In late summer, large bunches of dark-blue fruits, whitened with a dense waxy bloom, replace the flower clusters. The berries are sour when eaten raw, but make excellent jelly, syrup, or wine. Native Americans made a drink from the berries and also dried them for winter use. Flutes were made from the branches and they called the blue elderberry the "tree of music." The foliage is highly prized by deer and, consequently, most blue elderberry plants at Bryce Canyon are heavily browsed. CB

QUAKING ASPEN

Populus tremuloides   **Willow Family**

The smooth, greenish white bark of the younger quaking aspen trees is the most distinguishing characteristic. Quaking aspen trees are slender and have gracefully pendulous branches with finely-toothed, round-ovate leaves. The leaves have flat petioles, which cause them to tremble or quake in the slightest breeze. The trees typically occur in dense stands on moist hillsides and grow from root sprouts. Seedlings seldom develop into trees in this area under present climatic conditions, reproduction being mostly by suckers from established root systems. CB

NATIONAL PARK SERVICE

WHITE FIR

Abies concolor   **Pine Family**

The white fir is the most abundant tree in the montane forests of southern Utah. Young trees grow rapidly and are conical in outline. At maturity, the trees may attain heights of 100 to 120 feet and have dense, irregular crowns. The bark on young tree trunks is smooth and gray, but becomes thick and hard, deeply fissured into scaly ridges with age. The needles are borne singly and are flat, blunt, and curve upward. The cones are dark brown and borne upright on the branches. The scales of the cones drop off, leaving the central axis attached to the tree for some time. The trees are susceptible to a number of diseases, such as heart rot, which diminishes the value of the tree for lumber purposes. At Bryce Canyon, the white fir trees have had an infestation of an insect, the needle miner moth, which reached epidemic proportions in the 1950s. Many trees succumbed from extreme defoliation, while others were weakened and died later, or were left deformed.

DAWN M. GATHERUM

DOUGLAS FIR

Pseudotsuga menziesii **Pine Family**

Douglas fir trees are tall and have thick, deeply fissured, dark-brown bark and drooping branches. The needle-like leaves are spreading, flattened and flexible with very short petioles. The cones are easily identified by having the distinctive 3-pointed bracts that protrude beyond the thin, rounded cone scales. The cones are narrowly egg-shaped and hang downward. Douglas fir does not grow as large in the southwestern U. S. as it does in the Northwest, where it is the most valuable timber tree. In the Utah mountains, the tree does not occur in pure stands, but is commonly found growing with fir, spruce, pine, and aspen. It is reported that Native Americans and early settlers made a hot drink from the tender young needles of Douglas fir for use as a substitute for coffee.

BLUE SPRUCE

Picea pungens   **Pine Family**

An attractive conifer of moist sites at Bryce Canyon is the state tree of Utah, the blue spruce. The branches are borne in definite whorls and are stout and horizontal. The needles are bluish green, rigid, very sharp-pointed, square in cross-section, and are attached to peg-like projections from the twigs. These needles tend to extend at right anges from all sides of the twigs. The cones hang downward from the upper branches and drop intact from the tree after the seeds are dispersed. Since the seedlings of the tree do not adapt to the moderate or heavy grazing use of the forests, they appear practically absent from the forests of southern Utah outside the national parks. The blue spruce is widely cultivated as an ornamental tree.

SEGO LILY

Calochortus nuttallii   **Lily Family**

The name sego lily comes from a Shoshone Indian name for the plant. Closely related species are called mariposa lilies. The plant was sacred in Native American legend. The use of the bulb for food by the Native Americans was adopted by the early Mormon pioneers as well as by hunters and miners. The Native Americans gathered the bulbs in large quantities, using only a digging stick that had been sharpened and hardened in the fire. This very attractive plant was chosen as the state flower of Utah. The three large, waxy petals each have distinctive crescent-shaped, purplish markings and a fringe of bright yellow hairs on the inner surface. The leaves are grass-like, few in number, and are already withered by flowering time. Sego lily thrives in dry conditions, such as openings in the fir forest at Bryce Canyon.

STARLILY

Leucocrinum montanum   **Lily Family**

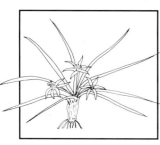

One of the most delicate and impressive wildflowers is the starlily, which dots the forest floor at Bryce Canyon during the month of June. The leaves are tufted and grass-like, surrounding one or more small, fragrant flowers. Each flower has a long floral tube, the base of which is below ground. Each floral tube bears six long, pure white petals, which are linear in outline and sharp-pointed. The stamens in the center of the flower are bright yellow in color. These lilies thrive in sandy to rocky, well-drained soil, often in thick litter under the conifer trees.

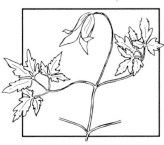

ROCKY MOUNTAIN CLEMATIS

Clematis columbiana   **Buttercup Family**

The trailing or climbing stems of the Rocky Mountain clematis are often found among shrubs or low trees, or may even spread out on the surface of the ground. The leaves are divided and made up of three leaflets, which are deeply cleft or toothed. The sepals of the nodding flowers are purple or blue in color, very thin, and spread outward at the tips. Stamens and pistils within the flower are very numerous. Later in the summer, the many tiny fruits that develop from the flower each have long, feathery parts for wind dispersal of the seeds.

Subalpine Open, Semi-moist Meadows

s one approaches Cedar Breaks National Monument from the east across the higher parts of the Markagunt Plateau, the "savannah" aspect of the vegetation is impressive. The forest is not continuous over the gradual slopes of the top of the plateau since the trees occupy only part of the total areas. Outcroppings and fairly recent lava beds are common, on which biological succession is barely beginning to form soil. Open, sunlit meadows cover many hillsides between the clumps of trees and extend into the lowest parts of the valleys. Colorful wildflowers cover these semi-moist meadows.

The greater portion of the Markagunt Plateau has suffered a high level of grazing pressure from domestic livestock for approximately 100 years. In contrast, however, the small area of Cedar Breaks National Monument that has had protection from grazing during the past fifty years has enjoyed the rejuvenation of wildflowers within its fenced areas. The open, semi-moist meadows present an almost incomparable display of color and variety for the visitor in late June to mid-August. Since the winter snows are generally heavy at this high elevation and do not all melt until late in June or early July, the plants have adapted to a short growing season, cool nights in summer, full sunlight, frequent summer thunderstorms, and occasional drought. The race to ripen seeds before winter comes is intense, and the seeds, once produced and scattered, face problems of germination and seedling survival under varying environmental conditions.

MARKAGUNT PENSTEMON

*Penstemon
leiophyllus*
Figwort Family

A characteristic
wildflower of the
open meadows at
Cedar Breaks is
this large-flowered
species of
penstemon. It may
grow up to 2 feet
in height in other
places, but at Cedar
Breaks, it is usually less than 15 inches tall. It often grows in clumps
and is very attractive from late July
until the end of the growing season
with its display of numerous blue to
purple flowers. The flowers are
tubular in shape and remind one of
snapdragons. The leaves are long and
narrow and are borne opposite along
the stem. This is the most abundant
penstemon at Cedar Breaks.

RYDBERG PENSTEMON

Penstemon rydbergii
Figwort Family

The Rydberg penstemon
plants are more or less
tufted and grow from
woody rhizomes. The
tubular flowers are blue
to purple in color and
persist for some time during the blooming period
of late summer. The
flowers occur in clumps
along the stem, each
clump having many small flowers, which
project out from all sides of the stem in
separate clusters. The leaves are lance-
shaped, opposite, few along the stem, and
mostly basal. The name penstemon means
"five stamens." Four of the stamens are
fertile, but the fifth stamen is represented
by a long, sterile filament, often densely
covered with hair. Penstemons are commonly found in meadows and open slopes.

FIREWEED

Epilobium angustifolium
Evening Primrose Family

The fireweed is not as tall at Cedar Breaks as it is at lower elevations, where it may attain heights of 6 feet. Although it is relatively diminutive at Cedar Breaks, it is nevertheless extremely attractive with its showy, rose to lilac-colored flowers in terminal, spike-like clusters. The flowers are 4-petaled and clawed. The lower flowers of the elongated cluster bloom first and the upper ones bloom later. As a result a plant may have long seed pods, open flowers, and buds in the same flower cluster at the same time. The leaves are lance-shaped and resemble those of the willow. The stalk, when split open, exposes a sweet, glutinous substance, which is said to be palatable. The plants grow in dense patches and often invade soil that has been disturbed by fire or cultivation.

YELLOW EVENING PRIMROSE *Oenothera flava* **Evening Primrose Family**

This stunning plant often occurs in areas where the soil has been disturbed, such as roadsides. It is a biennial plant, which has grayish foliage due to many fine, short hairs covering the surfaces of leaves and stems. The striking feature of the plant is the flower, which has a corolla tube that flares out into four huge, bright yellow lobes. The flowers are bright and crisp in early morning, but soon wither in the sun later in the day, as is common with evening primroses. Within the elongated corolla tube are the eight stamens and the stigma, which is divided into four stigma lobes. The old flowers of the previous day lie crinkled and fading to pinkish color among the basal rosette of dandelion-shaped leaves.

SCARLET PAINTBRUSH
Castilleja miniata
Figwort Family

The scarlet tufts of this paintbrush add a brilliant splash of color to the subdued green aspect of a small meadow among the trees, and whole expanses of open meadows may be vividly brightened with numerous blossoms. With the corollas of the flowers relatively inconspicuous, it is the sepals and colored bracts around the flowers that provide the showy colors of the plant. The plants are perennial with few stems and are erect from a woody base, which is often branched. Even though the plants have both chlorophyll for photosynthesis and an adequate root system for absorption of water and minerals, they are often partially parasitic on other plants through natural root-grafting.

ORANGE SNEEZEWEED *Dugaldia hoopesii* **Sunflower Family**

Limited areas of the open, sunlit meadows of Cedar Breaks have large clusters of a perennial plant that is very conspicuous during midsummer. The lance-shaped leaves are borne alternately along stems, which grow to about 3 feet in height. The flower heads are rather large in size and are vivid in color. The golden-yellow ray flowers radiate from a large cluster of darker, orange-brown disk flowers. Often the ray flowers are tinged with purple. Each of the ray flowers is tri-lobed at the tip. The plant contains a toxic glucoside which causes "spewing sickness" in sheep. It is also poisonous to cattle, but is rarely eaten by them.

OREGON FLEABANE *Erigeron speciosus* **Sunflower Family**

The fleabanes, often pale in colors, look like delicate, downy daisies. There are many species of fleabanes and they bloom earlier than the asters. They are usually at their peak in early summer, whereas asters flower mostly in late summer and fall. Typically, fleabanes have twice as many ray flowers as asters. The ray flowers are the silky fringe of the flower head and the disk flowers are always yellow. The fleabanes generally have a long blooming period.

PRAIRIE SMOKE
Geum triflorum
Rose Family

The stem of the pink-colored flower of the prairie smoke bends over, causing the flower to hang downward. There are common-ly many flower stalks in a cluster. Both the sepals and petals are pink or whitish purple in color. As the plant matures the styles of the flowers elongate and become featherlike. When released, the long, feathery style acts as a sail to disperse the seed into the wind. The leaves, being compound and finely dissected, are mostly basal and fernlike. New sprouts appear in early summer as soon as the snowbanks retreat. The roots of the plant were boiled by Native Americans to make a beverage, which is said to taste much like sassafras tea.

LEAFY-BRACT ASTER   *Aster foliaceus*   **Sunflower Family**

One of the most striking of all the asters, this perennial occurs in many high alpine meadows. Erect stems develop from a creeping rootstalk. The leaves are mostly entire or have smooth margins. The bracts around the base of the flower heads overlap like shingles on a roof in the asters, which contrasts to the single row of bracts around the base of the flower heads in the fleabanes. Also, the ray flowers are broader in the aster and fewer in number. The stems of the leafy-bract aster are commonly tinged with red. Where the plants occur on rangeland, they are highly preferred by grazing animals, especially sheep.

WESTERN ASTER

Aster occidentalis
Sunflower Family

Several rather stout stems arise from a slender, branching rhizome to a height of about 10 inches. The leaves have smooth margins and are narrowly lance-shaped. The flower heads have dark lavender, ray flowers, radiating out of a small cluster of bright yellow disk flowers. At Cedar Breaks, the western aster and the leafy-bract aster cover wide expanses of open, sunlit meadows in mid- and late-summer months, remaining in bloom until the very last of the growing season.

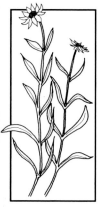

LITTLE SUNFLOWER   *Helianthella uniflora*   **Sunflower Family**

The flowering heads of the little sunflower are usually solitary on stems that are 1 to 2 feet tall. The stems arise from a woody rootstalk and are often covered with numerous flattened hairs. The basal leaves are numerous and shaped like large spatulas. The stem leaves are reduced in size and number. The flower heads resemble those of the common sunflower but are smaller. The ray flowers are yellow to brownish-purple in color. The plants bloom profusely in rocky soil on the steeper slopes of the open meadows.

COMMON DANDELION   *Taraxacum officinale*   **Sunflower Family**

The common dandelion is probably the most universal of all plants due to the ease with which the seeds are scattered and taken by man to all parts of the earth. The heads of yellow ray flowers are borne on leafless, hollow stalks and develop very early in the growing season, in contrast to most flowers of the sunflower family, which bloom in late summer or autumn. The yellow heads are in striking contrast to the bright green foliage. The leaves are elongate and coarsely toothed. The common dandelion is one of the best known and least appreciated flowers in the world. The plant was probably introduced into the mountains of southern Utah through grazing activities of the past century, and it is one of the best wildlife food sources for upland birds, deer, and other animals.

ELKWEED

Frasera speciosa   **Gentian Family**

A plant that favors rich soil in open, evergreen forests is the conspicuous elkweed. The first year of this biennial is a cluster of large, broad, light-green colored leaves. The mature plant of the second year is a single, coarse, erect, unbranched stem with increasingly small and narrow leaves toward the top. The flower stalk has numerous greenish white flowers spotted with purple and may attain heights up to 5 feet. Many insects in search of nectar visit the flowers, which bloom all summer. The brown, sturdy stalk of this plant can be seen standing erect, resisting the drifting snow until late winter.

MOUNTAIN MEADOW THICKLEAF GROUNDSEL

FEW-FLOWERED GOLDENROD

Senecio crassulus
Sunflower Family

The groundsels comprise a large group of plants that are similar in appearance but are difficult to identify as to species. As a group, they may be distinguished by bracts in a single series beneath the flower head. Several stems arise from a loosely-branched rootstalk, which bears mostly spatula-shaped basal leaves. The stem leaves are few in number and reduced in size. The small, attractive flower heads are in clusters. The plant is rather woolly and the bracts under the flower head look as though they were covered with fur. When the plant goes to seed, long, white hairs develop for wind transport of the seed. A toxin produced by some groundsels causes liver damage and is called "stomach staggers" in grazing animals.

Solidago sparsiflora
Sunflower Family

Ancient physicians believed that goldenrod had healing powers, which explains the name *Solidago*, meaning to "solidify" or "to make whole." The few-flowered goldenrod is perennial and comes from a branching rootstalk. The ray flowers are very small and are yellow in color as are the disk flowers. The plants are commonly only about 1 foot in height and inhabit sunny locations.

YELLOW SALSIFY

Tragopogon dubius   **Sunflower Family**

The salsifies are Old World species that were introduced to America by the early colonists as a food source, and have spread rapidly from cultivated areas into the mountains. The bright yellow flower heads are composed of only ray flowers, which open in early morning but close toward mid-day. More conspicuous than the flower heads are the huge, round, white seed heads that form when the plant matures. Each seed has a stalk that bears a featherlike growth that expands in dry weather to form a miniature parachute. The plants possess milky juice. The roots, when cooked, taste somewhat like oysters. The coagulated juice of the plant was chewed by early settlers as a remedy for indigestion. (BC)

MOUNTAIN DANDELION
Agoseris glauca
Sunflower Family

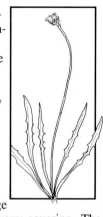

This native wildflower resembles the common dandelion, having a basal rosette of leaves, a leafless flower stalk, and a single head of yellow ray flowers. The flower head is more slender, and the leaves are much narrower than those of the common dandelion. The foliage has a light-colored, waxy covering. The thick, milky juice that is released when the tissues are broken turns dark upon exposure to the air and contains a certain amount of rubber. Native Americans chewed the solidified juice. The plants are highly preferred by grazing animals, especially sheep. The flowers change in color from yellow to purplish as they mature. The seeds are distributed by the wind. (BC)

LANCELEAF GOLDENWEED   *Halopappus lanceolatus*   Sunflower Family

Growing on well-drained sites in the forest openings at Cedar Breaks are many composites, including the lanceleaf goldenweed. Several stems grow from a branched rootstalk. Leaves are alternately attached along the stem. The flowering heads are smaller than those of the common sunflower, and the disk flowers are yellow in color. The common sunflower has brown disk flowers, is of European origin, and does not occur at this high elevation in our mountains.

LEOPARD LILY

MOUNTAIN OR LOW GOLDENROD

Fritillaria atropurpurea
Lily Family

The most distinctive
feature of the leopard lily
is the coloring of the
flower. The flowers are
broadly bell shaped and
hang downward from un-
branched stems. The in-
ner surfaces of the sepals
and petals are dull
purplish brown with
greenish yellow spots.
The flower is often overlooked because of
its coloring and the way it hangs downward
to effectively hide the other flower parts.
The unbranched stem comes from an
underground corm, which also supports
grass-like leaves. The corms are starchy
and were used for food by the Native
Americans.

Solidago multiradiata
Sunflower Family

Rounded clusters of
small flower heads
typify the low
goldenrod. Each
head has separate
disk and ray
flowers. The plants
grow from 4 to 6
inches tall. The
leaves are simple
and are borne
singly at each node. When you see
the goldenrods in bloom you know
that summer has passed its peak, and
that fall will soon arrive. Goldenrods
are not palatable to animals, inasmuch
as they contain small quantities of
rubber latex.

PENNYCRESS, WILD CANDYTUFT
Thlaspi montanum   **Mustard Family**

Because this small, white-flowered pennycress blooms early in
the season before the larger flowers of other plants are
blooming to dominate the scene, it is conspicuous even though
individual plants are very small. Some leaves form a basal
rosette at ground level and others clasp the stems that arise
from the branching rootstalk. The leaves are smooth and dark
green in color. The flowers have 4 white petals and 6 stamens.
Thick clusters of the flowers borne terminally give a bed of
plants a tufted appearance. The flowers develop into strongly-
flattened, triangular pods.

LANCELEAF SPRINGBEAUTY   *Claytonia lanceolata*   **Purslane Family**

One of the first tiny, pink flowers to appear in the spring soon after the snowdrifts disappear is the lanceleaf springbeauty. The plants grow from a round underground corm with a basal leaf and only one pair of opposite stem leaves. The corms are edible and were used by the Native Americans for food. The flower has two sepals, five petals, and five stamens. The flower petals vary from dark pink to light pink to white with pink-colored veins. The lance-shaped leaves are dark-colored and shiny and provide an attractive contrast to the colorful blossoms.

RED ELDERBERRY   *Sambucus racemosa*   **Honeysuckle Family**

An attractive display is provided throughout the summer by the red elderberry. In early summer, the rounded masses of small, white flowers crown the foliage of bright green compound leaves. In late summer these many flowers are replaced by shiny, scarlet berries. The fruits of this species are not edible as are the fruits of other elderberries. Cases of poisoning have been reported from eating the berries and other parts of this shrub. The compound leaves are opposite in attachment to the stem and are made up of 7 leaflets with sharply toothed edges. The stems are pithy.

Subalpine Marshy Meadows

he breathtaking floral display of Cedar Breaks National Monument is most exquisite and colorful in the subalpine marshy meadows. These bog-like areas are very limited in size, but are often found closely adjacent to the fir-spruce forest, or are completely surrounded by semi-moist meadows. They appear along drainage systems on the Markagunt Plateau. The boundary between the marshy meadows and adjacent plant communities is a rather stable area, being determined by the soil factor of saturated soil or soil with water covering the surface.

The abundant moisture throughout the growing season permits lush growth of plants with striking colors, such as shooting star, bistort, Parry primrose, monkshood, pretty Jacob's ladder, elephanthead, and the exquisite meadow gentian. Several of these lovely wildflowers emit disagreeable odors when disturbed, which is incongruous with their appearance. The marshy meadows are limited in size and are surrounded by better-drained meadows or clusters of subalpine forest trees. The species of wildflowers from these very wet meadows do not persist in the surrounding, better-drained habitats.

NATIONAL PARK SERVICE

HEARTLEAF BITTERCRESS
Cardamine cordifolia   **Mustard Family**

The heartleaf bittercress is an erect, perennial plant. Several simple flowering stems come from an extensively developed, slender rhizome and bear simple, smooth leaves, most of which are attached upward on the stem and not as a basal rosette. The stems grow from 12 to 14 inches tall and are sometimes branched. The flowers are often so numerous that they create a very effective display. There are 4 petals to each flower, as is true of all members of the mustard family.

NATIONAL PARK SERVICE

PLANTAINLEAF BUTTERCUP

BOG VIOLET

*Ranunculus
alismifolius*
Buttercup Family

An early blooming
buttercup in very
moist mountain
meadows is the plan-
tainleaf buttercup. It
often covers large
areas of wet meadows
with golden color in early summer. This is
the only buttercup that has the combination
of a 10-petaled flower and undivided
leaves. The fruiting heads that develop
from the flowers are very narrow.

Viola nephrophylla
Violet Family

The bog
violet is
widespread
throughout
North America.
It is an impres-
sive violet with heart-shaped leaves. It
grows in open, moist meadows or shaded
sites in forests. It is a stemless, compact
plant that grows up to 6 inches tall from
a rather fleshy rootstalk. The flowers are
purple and are about 1/2 inch in
diameter. The coloring of the petals is
distinctive, with petals pale in color near
the base and deeply colored toward the
edges. The lowest petal has a spur, and
all petals have dark purple veins.

PARRY PRIMROSE

MONKSHOOD

Primula parryi
Primrose Family

The large leaves up to 1 foot in length grow in a rosette at the base of the stem of this large and showy primrose. The flowers are in a somewhat rounded terminal cluster of 3 to 12 flowers per stalk. Each flower has a bell-shaped calyx and a five-parted narrow corolla tube of deep rose-pink color. The flowers and the foliage have a disagreeably strong odor. The plants may be found in wet marshes at Cedar Breaks and also near the summit of Brian Head, clustered in somewhat sheltered places at the base of large rocks or cliffs. Apparently, there is enough moisture retained in these habitats near timberline to accommodate these water-loving primroses.

Aconitum columbianum
Buttercup Family

One of the tallest plants of wet meadows, and also the one with the deepest blue or purple flowers, is the monkshood. The stems are from 1 to 4 feet tall with hooded flowers widely spaced among them. There are only two little, hammer-like petals in the flower, both of them housed comfortably under a curious, peaked hood that resembles those worn by medieval monks. The leaves are incised and toothed, resembling those of the geranium. All parts of the plant are poisonous due to the presence of alkaloids, but the roots and seeds are especially poisonous. A heart and nerve sedative is obtained from the roots of the plant. Monkshood is truly a mountaineer plant, requiring soil coolness and plenty of moisture.

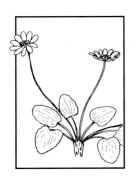

MARSH MARIGOLD   *Caltha leptosepala*   **Buttercup Family**

Large, white and gold flowers on plants that love to "keep their feet wet" characterize the marsh marigold. Petals are missing, the white parts being sepals. The numerous stamens in the center of the flower are bright yellow in color. The flowers are from 1 to 2 inches broad. The leaves are all basal, roughly oval in shape, with heart-shaped bases. The Native Americans use the roots of marsh marigold as a potherb after washing and cooking away the poisons. Cattle have been poisoned by eating the plant.

MEADOW GENTIAN
Gentianopsis detonsa
Gentian Family

The flowers of the meadow gentian close up under cloudy skies, but to find masses of them fully open on a sunny day, displaying their fringed petals, is a reward to all who visit the wet meadows of high mountains. Subalpine meadows may at such times become a waving mass of deep-blue color. Each flower is at the end of a stem that bears several pairs of oblong, opposite leaves. The corolla tube forms a rather square column for over half the total length of the petals. Most gentians occur in cool, mountainous parts of the earth.

MOUNTAIN DEATHCAMAS

Zigadenus elegans
Lily Family

The whole plant of the mountain deathcamas is poisonous. Early settlers of the Southwest occasionally mistook the bulbs of deathcamas for those of camas, onion, or sego lily—with disastrous results. Livestock are poisoned by eating the foliage. The cream-colored flowers are grouped at the top of straight, slender stems, which spring from a clump of stiff, bluish green leaves. The flowers are usually about 1/2 inch in diameter. At the base of each petal and sepal there is a greenish spot. The stamens have black anthers.

AMERICAN BISTORT
Polygonum bistortoides
Buckwheat Family

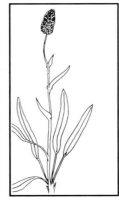

Large areas of the meadows of Cedar Breaks, from a distance, appear to be covered with tufts of cotton on slender stalks. Upon closer inspection the "blossoms" are found to be the terminal clusters of tiny, white or pale rose-colored flowers, which have a sweet, nauseating odor. The leaves are narrow and tapering; the upper ones small and sessile and the lower ones petioled. The root is thick, twisted, and snakelike. The root of the bistort has been used by many people for food. Native Americans made soups and stews from it, or roasted it on coals. It is also eaten by various wild animals.

PRETTY SHOOTING STAR   *Dodecatheon pulchellum*   **Primrose Family**

From a basal cluster of spatula-shaped leaves, the stems of the pretty shooting star grow to about 10 inches tall. These stems bear a crown of delicately perfumed, magenta-colored blossoms at their summits. The petals are swept backward like a coronet. The dark purplish stamens are united and exposed at a slender point. These plants are often found in large masses in rather wet meadow soils. The nodding flowers with reflexed petals set the shooting star apart as one of the most striking and beautiful of all flowers.

ELEPHANTHEAD
Pedicularis groenlandica
Figwort Family

Growing in marshy mountain meadows is one of the most interesting flowers of our mountains. A dense spike of small, red-purple to pink flowers rises from a stem 8 to 15 inches tall above a basal rosette of fern-like dark green leaves. The upper petal of each tiny flower forms a long, down-curved tube, having a comical resemblance to an elephant's trunk. Other flower parts resemble the forehead and ears of an elephant. These plants are found in the western part of the United States.

PARRY LOUSEWORT, RAM'S HORN
Pedicularis parryi
Figwort Family

The Parry lousewort has erect stems 4 to 12 inches tall and bears stalks of small, pale yellow flowers. The leaves are somewhat fern-like, being divided nearly to the midrib into toothed segments. The flowers have an upper lip that is open and hood-shaped. The genus name is from Latin and means "louse." Seeds from some species of these plants were used in ancient times to kill lice, which explains the common name lousewort. "Wort" is an old Saxon term referring to plant.

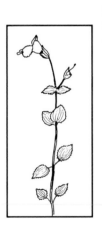

COMMON MONKEY FLOWER   *Mimulus guttatus*   **Figwort Family**

Monkey flowers are among our most appealing, yet most variable, wild plants. The dark green leaves are opposite each other on the stem and are often sticky. The corolla of the flower is about an inch in length with a closed throat. The flowers are yellow spotted with red and are two-lipped. The stems are from 5 inches to 2 feet in height and are weak and rather succulent. When the plants fall down to touch the wet soil, the stems often develop roots at the nodes. The plants grow in wet places, as in the water at the edges of brooks and streams.

PRETTY JACOB'S LADDER

Polemonium pulcherrimum   **Phlox Family**

The leaves of the pretty Jacob's ladder are somewhat fern-like, having elliptical leaflets that are 2-ranked, suggesting a ladder. The plants are from 2 to 3 feet tall and bear a number of wide, open, pale blue flowers. The blue petals spread out wide and the flower as a whole is bell-shaped. The leaves have a strong and very disagreeable odor, somewhat like the odor of a skunk.

ESCHSCHOLTZ BUTTERCUP
Ranunculus eschscholtzii   **Buttercup Family**

A moist meadow near timberline on a mountain is an ideal habitat for the Eschscholtz buttercup. The name *Ranunculus* means "little frog" and the name "buttercup" refers to the resemblance of the smooth, shiny petals to freshly churned butter. The Eschscholtz buttercup plants are especially smooth and shiny. The yellow flowers vary from 1/2 to 1 inch in diameter. The upper leaves are divided into long, finger-like leaflets, whereas the lower leaves are smaller and simple, with toothed and lobed margins.

Timberline Forests

he trees in the subalpine or timberline forests are grouped closely together within groves, leaving extensive unforested areas between groves, which are occupied in full sunlight by the two previously described meadow communities at Cedar Breaks. Such a clustered forest growth is referred to as savannah. The subalpine fir and Engelmann spruce trees are relatively small, narrow, and spire-topped. The compact groups of trees often contain one or a few big seed trees surrounded by younger offspring. Perennial flowering plants, springing from woody root-crowns, have special advantages here. Among the clumped trees, the wildflowers often grow lush and tall, such as wild parsley, columbine, larkspur, bluebells, and lupine. Shrubs such as gooseberry currant and twinberry often form dense thickets in such forests.

At its lower altitudinal limits, the subalpine fir-Engelmann spruce forest has numerous aspen groves. Aspen is an early stage of forest succession, providing shade and increasing moisture conditions to help establish the climax stage of succession, the conifers.

In very exposed sites, such as on the windswept ridges of Cedar Breaks and on the upper portions of Brian Head, both subalpine fir and Engelmann spruce become dwarfed and bush-like instead of tall, stately, and arrowly pyramid-shaped in outline. The branches become gnarled and twisted instead of straight and horizontal from erect trunks. This "krumholz," or flag-formed woody vegetation, is typical of timberline conditions, typified by harsh winds blowing frost particles against anything that projects above the snowdrifts of winter. The soils of these high elevations in the mountains are very thin and fragile, easily damaged by overgrazing or excessive human use.

ASPEN BLUEBELL

Mertensia arizonica   **Borage Family**

Aspen bluebells cover large areas among the spruce and fir trees, often forming large clumps. The numerous flowers are pendant from the upper parts of drooping stems. The narrow, bell-shaped flowers flare open and hang downward. The flowers are lavender-blue in color and develop from pink buds. The smooth leaves grow alternately along the stems. The plants are among the most lush wildflowers of the high mountains.

SUBALPINE LARKSPUR

HEARTLEAF ARNICA

Delphinium occidentale
Buttercup Family

Subalpine larkspur is often found growing in dense clumps. The stems may be 4 feet in height at Cedar Breaks and are crowned with very dark purple flowers in open, elongated clusters. Each flower is very distinct, having 5 deeply colored sepals. One of the sepals forms a spur into which nectar-bearing spurs of the two upper petals project. The 4 petals may not be as deeply colored as the sepals. There are many stamens in the flower. The leaves are palmately lobed or deeply divided. The plants may be poisonous to livestock, especially cattle.

Arnica cordifolia
Sunflower Family

Heartleaf arnica has the largest flower heads of all species of arnica. The flower heads are borne singly on stems that bear op-posite heart-shaped leaves. The leaves are slightly hairy, glandular, and gray-green in color. Fibrous underground stems connect stands of arnica in open fir and spruce forests. The flowers bloom in early summer and develop seed heads that have tufts of white pappus. All parts of the plant have medicinal value, but the flowers are most potent. A drug obtained from the plant causes a rise in body temperature if given orally or intravenously. When applied externally to wounds, it aids in preventing infection. (BC)

SILVERY LUPINE
Lupinus argenteus
Legume Family

Because horizontal rootstalks are developed, the silvery lupine spreads out to form large clumps or patches of plants that grow up to 30 inches tall at the time of flowering. The flower stalks bear numerous blue or blue and white colored flowers. Large areas of open meadows near forest boundaries are filled with masses of blue color in midsummer. The leaflets of each leaf radiate out in a fingerlike fashion. Hairs are numerous on the lower leaflet surfaces, but the upper surfaces are smooth and shiny green.

RICHARDSON GERANIUM
Geranium richardsonii
Geranium Family

The white-flowered Richardson geranium is a woodland species usually restricted to groves of fir, spruce, or aspen. It grows up to 3 feet tall and has delicate, white flowers with conspicuous veins. The 10 stamens of the flower are united at the base to form a short tube. The flowers develop into a long beak, which forms the seeds at the base. The leaves are large and palmately lobed, resembling those of larkspur and monkshood. Each lobe is further toothed into a distinctive pattern. The plants thrive in moist, rich soil of the forest. (BC)

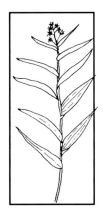

STARRY FALSE SOLOMONSEAL

Smilicina stellata **Lily Family**

Numerous lance-shaped leaves are
borne on stems that arise from
slender, underground rootstalks to
form dense patches of starry false
solomonseal in the forest. Early in
the summer, the unbranched stems
terminate in racemes of many
white flowers that look like
6-pointed stars. The berries are
pale green and marked with
blackish-red stripes. The young
shoots and leaves may be used for
greens. Sheep often graze on the
leaves and stems.

SUBALPINE FIR

Abies lasiocarpa   **Pine Family**

DAWN M. GATHERUM

The dominant timberline tree of Cedar Breaks is the subalpine fir, a stately spire that grows to heights of about 90 feet. It is a slow-growing tree with a narrow crown and short, stiff branches. The lower branches usually droop somewhat. At very high elevations, the subalpine fir may be dwarfed and shrub-like. The cones are dark purple, upright, and deciduous. The bark is thin, grayish, and becomes fissured and scaly in over-maturity. The needles are rather short, flattened, dull at the tips, and radially arranged on the branches, but tend to grow upward, away from gravity. It is reported that Native Americans made a medicinal tea from the needles and resinous blisters of the tree.

ENGELMANN SPRUCE

Picea engelmanii   **Pine Family**

A forest of Engelmann spruce usually contains trees of all ages and sizes because the seedlings and young trees are able to grow in the dense shade and upon the thick litter of the older trees. The trees have a shallow root system and are often blown over by the strong winds that frequently develop at high elevations in mountains. The tree is narrowly pyramidal in outline and bears needles that are acute, but very sharp to the touch. The cones are papery at maturity and hang downward on the branches. The cones fall in winter after the seeds are scattered. Twigs of spruces are roughened by persistent leaf bases, which are conspicuous after the older needles have been replaced by growth of new needles. Engelmann spruce makes a fair timber tree since the lumber is rather light in weight and close-grained.

COMMON JUNIPER

Juniperus communis   **Cypress Family**

In contrast to the other native junipers, the common juniper is not a tree, but rather a spreading shrub, often found in the understory of high mountain forests. It may form dense thickets of tangled branches. The leaves are needle-shaped, very sharp-pointed, and slightly curved. The berry-like cones are globose, blue, and covered with a white bloom. Several varieties of common juniper are used in landscaping. (BC)

COLORADO COLUMBINE   *Aquilegia caerulea*   **Buttercup Family**

The most distinctive and attractive flower of the spruce-fir forest at Cedar Breaks is the Colorado columbine. The large flowers have petal-like sepals that are either creamy white or tinged with blue. The five petals each have a slender spur that extends backward between the sepals. The basal leaves are compound with rounded lobes that are cleft. Columbines are not important forage plants, but on overgrazed ranges, sheep graze them heavily and they are becoming rare in areas where they were once abundant. The great numbers of plants at Cedar Breaks results from the protection of the area from grazing by domestic animals since the national monument was created.   (BC)

CANADA VIOLET
Viola canadensis
Violet Family

Rich, moist soil in the spruce-fir groves of Cedar Breaks offer the best conditions for growth of the Canada violet. The stems are weak but often grow over a foot tall and the stems bear smooth, heart-shaped leaves. The flower stalks develop from the leaf axils and the flowers are white with purple veins. As is true of most violets, the early-blooming showy flowers do not form seeds, but are followed by inconspicuous flowers that are fertile. The seeds may be scattered far from the plant that formed them by seed-pods that burst violently at maturity.

SOUTHERN LIGUSTICUM
Ligusticum porteri
Parsley Family

A robust plant that often reaches 3 feet in height with flowers that resemble Queen Anne's lace is the southern ligusticum. The plants may be found in open meadows, but are typically found in the forested areas. The leaves are fern-like and numerous. The flowers are white and grow in flat-topped clusters. A pungent odor given off by the leaves and stems resembles the odor of celery. Native Americans used the "Osha" roots to treat a myriad of illnesses, including upset stomach, pneumonia, rheumatism, headaches, and snakebites. Grazing animals find the plant palatable.

Alpine Tundra on Brian Head

rom timberline on Brian Head Mountain to the summit, the climate is too severe for any trees to survive. The strong winds, especially in winter, become the limiting factor for forest development. The winds drift the snow, leaving bare areas exposed to the extremely low winter temperatures. At timberline, however, the strong winds blow snow and ice crystals against the upper portion of the tree trunks that happen to project above snow drifts to dessicate and destroy the buds and needles, thus limiting the development of normal tree growth. Soil forms very slowly on this rocky summit, primarily in narrow crevices between the rocks. Mosses, lichens, sedges, and dwarf grasses have been here for ages, all striving patiently to build humus. The spaces between the barren rocks often produce miniature flower gardens in summertime. The sedges, grasses, and other plants have full sunlight to themselves without tree competition. The ever-present adverse condition is low temperature accompanied by strong wind.

The summit is a land of tough dwarf plants, mostly perennials. Low, woody mats with basal leaves less than a few inches high are common patterns of vegetation. When spring finally comes with a rush to the alpine areas after the disappearance of snow banks in late June or early July, the dormant plants burst into life during the days of longest sunshine. Short shoots of new growth break from the ground with buds already formed. There seems to be an abundance of blossoms in porportion to the size and amount of foliage of the plants. By the end of July, the seed crop is largely mature, and by mid-August the browns and crimsons of fall colors spread a carpet over the heights. Some of the plants of this zone of harsh living conditions attain greater age than is normally reached by plants of lower vegetational belts. The mats or tufts of dwarfed plants with very thick, woody rootstalks give clues to the plant's longevity, since they have survived the snow cover of a great many alpine winters.

TUSHAR PAINTBRUSH
Castilleja parvula
Figwort Family

The actual flowers of the paintbrush are narrow, tubular, and greenish yellow. The flowers are partially enclosed by brightly colored, leafy bracts, which provide the colorful display. Some species have bright orange and red leafy bracts, such as those that are common in the meadows of Cedar Breaks. On the rocky slopes of higher mountains, a diminutive tushar paintbrush with dark red or almost purple leafy bracts can be found. The plants bloom throughout most of the short, timberline summer.

MOUNTAIN LOCOWEED   *Oxytropis oreophila*   Legume Family

A rather procumbent plant above timberline is the mountain locoweed. The stems curve upward somewhat and bear odd, pinnate leaves with numerous leaflets. At flowering time the calyx of the flower is a tube with 5 pointed teeth, which enlarges and splits open as the pod develops following flowering. The flower is somewhat purple and has the tip of the keel rounded. The plants bloom continuously so that buds, fully developed flowers, and pods can be found on the same plant at the same time. Many members of the legume family inhabit harsh and inhospitable environments, such as above timberline on mountains and in deserts.

ALPINE PRICKLY CURRANT
Ribes montigenum
Saxifrage Family

A low, densely-branched shrub that often forms thickets is the alpine prickly currant. The stems bear spines below the leaves and are usually prickly between the leaves as well. The leaves are fairly small, finely glandular, hairy, and deeply 3 or 5 lobed. The flowers occur several to a cluster and have tiny, red petals arranged in the shape of saucers. The berries are bright red and covered with gland-tipped hairs. Deer browse on the foliage and various birds utilize the berries. The berries are also used for jams and jellies.

CUSHION PHLOX
Phlox pulvinata
Phlox Family

Dense mats or cushions are formed by the cushion phlox. The leaves are almost needle-like in shape and are crowded closely together along the spreading stems. During summertime, the flowers nearly cover the surface of the compact cushion of stems and leaves. In the phlox, the corolla tubes flare at right angles to the tube. When the flower is held up to the light, the stamens can be seen at different heights in the tubes. The flowers are rather small and may be white or slightly bluish in color.

113

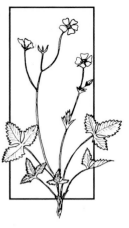

PRETTY CINQUEFOIL *Potentilla concinna* **Rose Family**

Cinquefoils have flowers that resemble those of the strawberry plant, but are usually yellow in color instead of white. The pretty cinquefoil has bright yellow, comparativel٠ small flowers. The foliage is covered with fine hairs. There are three leaflets in a com‑ pound leaf, the lower surface of the leaflets being white-felted. The plants are low and compact with fairly short stems and lie flat on the ground or across the rocks near the point where the plant is anchored in sparse soil between the rocks. (BC)

SULFUR BUCKWHEAT *Eriogonum umbellatum* **Buckwheat Family**

The sulfur buckwheat, a tough, long-lived plant, is well equipped to thrive in a rugged environment. The stalks are leafless and bear umbrella-shaped masses of bright yellow flowers. As the blossoms mature, they gradually change color from bright yellow to shades of orange and brown. The spatula-shaped leaves are white and fuzzy underneath but smooth and dull green on the upper surfaces. The tough, thick foliage and stout stems adapt the plant to harsh winds and to drought-like conditions during the growing season. (BC)

References

Abrams, L. 1940. *Illustrated Flora of the Pacific States,* Stanford University Press, Palo Alto, CA.

Albee, B. J., L. M. Schultz, and S. Goodrich, 1988. *Atlas of the Vascular Plants of Utah,* Salt Lake City, UT., Museum of Natural History Occasional Publication No. 7.

Anderson, B. A., and A. H. Holmgren, *Mountain Plants of Northeastern Utah,* Circular 319, Utah State University Extension Service, Logan, UT.

Arnberger, L. P., 1952. *Flowers of the Southwest Mountains,* Southwestern Monuments Assoc., Globe, AZ.

Bailey, V. L., and H. E. Bailey, 1949. *Woody Plants of the Western National Parks,* The University Press, Notre Dame, IN.

Craighead, J. J., F. C. Craighead, and R. J. Davis, 1963. *A Field Guide to Rocky Mountain Wildflowers,* Peterson Field Guide Series, Houghton Mifflin Co., Boston, MA.

Cronquist, A., A. H. Holmgren, N. H. Holmgren, and J. L. Reveal, 1972. *Intermountain Flora, Vascular Plants of the Intermountain West,* Vol. I, Hafner Publishing Company, Inc., New York and London.

Davis, R. J. 1952. *Flora of Idaho,* Brigham Young University Press, Provo, UT.

Harrington, H. D., 1954. *Manual of the Plants of Colorado,* Sage Books, Denver, CO.

Hitchcock, C. L., A. Cronquist, M. Ownbey, and J. W. Thompson, 1969. *Vascular Plants of the Pacific Northwest,* 5 parts, University of Washington Press, Seattle, WA.

Jepson, C. E., and L. F. Allen, 1958. *Wild Flowers of Zion and Bryce Canyon National Parks and Cedar Breaks National Monument,* Wheelwright Lithographing Co., Salt Lake City, UT.

Kearney, T. H., and R. H. Peebles, R. H., 1960. *Arizona Flora,* Second Edition, University of California Press, Berkeley, CA.

Nelson, R. A., 1976. *Plants of Zion National Park,* Zion Natural History Association, Deseret Press, Salt Lake City, UT.

Patraw, P. M., 1954. *Flowers of the Southwest Mesas,* Southwestern Monument Association, Globe, AZ.

Presnall, R., *Trees of the Canyon Country,* Bryce Canyon Natural History Association, Paragon Press, Inc., Salt Lake City, UT.

Rydberg, P. A., 1954. *Flora of the Rocky Mountains and Adjacent Plains,* Second Edition, Hafner, New York, NY.

Welsh, S. L., N. C. Atwood, S. Goodrich, and L. C. Higgins, 1987. *A Utah Flora,* Great Basin Naturalist Memoir 9: 1-894, Brigham Young University Press, Provo, UT.

Index

Index

Index

Index